First Month

Baby's
Birth Day : _____ / _____

AF270844

Growth and Development   Baby's weight/length : _____

❋ At birth baby can hear, smell, feel, taste, and can best see objects that are 8 to10 inches away.
❋ Baby will be awake only for brief periods of time.
❋ Baby's arm and leg movements are jerky, controlled mostly by reflexes.
❋ Baby will keep hands fisted and can only lift her head briefly.

This calendar gives general information on the events taking place during a baby's first year of life. It is not intended to take the place of your baby's health care. If you have any questions or concerns regarding your baby's health, call your baby's health care provider.

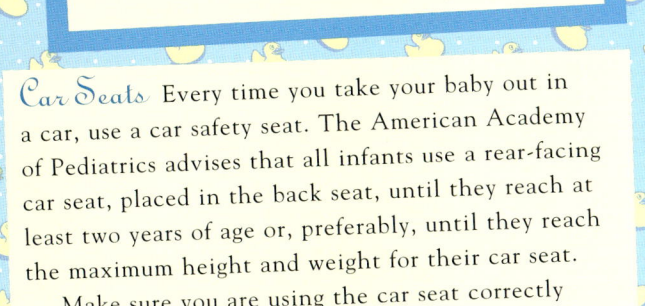

Car Seats Every time you take your baby out in a car, use a car safety seat. The American Academy of Pediatrics advises that all infants use a rear-facing car seat, placed in the back seat, until they reach at least two years of age or, preferably, until they reach the maximum height and weight for their car seat.

Make sure you are using the car seat correctly and that it is properly installed. Read the car seat instructions and your vehicle's owner's manual, and keep them in the car. Many local fire departments will check your car seat to make sure it is safe and secured properly.

Cars with air bags pose a significant hazard to children, so always buckle children in the back seat.

For more information, ask your baby's health care provider and check the car safety seat guidelines from the American Academy of Pediatrics at HealthyChildren.org.

Shaken Baby Syndrome All babies cry, sometimes inconsolably. Most crying is normal and healthy. Shaken Baby Syndrome (SBS) occurs when a baby is shaken violently out of frustration or anger by a caregiver in an attempt to stop the baby from crying. SBS can result in brain damage, blindness, and even death.

Never shake a baby! Make a plan for what to do when your baby is inconsolable and share your plan with your baby's other caregivers. Learn more at DontShake.org and CalmACryingBaby.org. (See How to Calm a Crying Baby on page 9.)

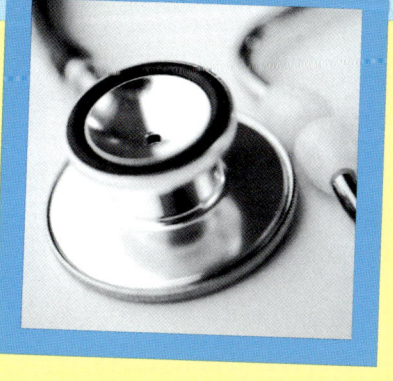

Nobody likes shots, especially nasty diseases — so don't miss a single vaccination.

At the Second Month Checkup, your baby will receive several immunizations. Immunizations are essential to your child's well-being and protect him from life-threatening diseases. There is a very slight risk of side effects associated with immunizations; be sure to discuss any questions or concerns you may have with your baby's health care provider.

Most immunizations are given in a series over several months and more than one dose is necessary to fully protect your child. So it is very important to keep your child up-to-date and not miss any doses. To help you keep track, fill in the Immunization Record on page 25.

Bottle-feeding Infant formulas are similar to breast milk and are available in three forms: powder, concentrate, and ready-to-use liquid. With any formula, be sure to follow the directions on the label exactly. If water is needed, do not add too little or too much, because your baby will not get the proper amount of nutrients and calories he needs. Your baby's health care provider can assist you in choosing the best formula for your baby.

Regular cow's milk should not be given in the first year because the kind of protein and fat it contains is too hard for babies to digest and may irritate the intestine. Ask your baby's health care provider when to switch to regular milk.

Feeding Tips Try to make feeding time a special time for you and your baby. Holding your baby promotes healthy emotional development. Lots of cuddling, talking, and singing helps your baby develop into a happy and secure child.

If you are bottle-feeding, resist the temptation to prop your baby's bottle. Hold the baby's head higher than the body so that the milk goes down his throat and doesn't pool around the eustachian tubes near his ears. This has been associated with an increase in ear infections.

Colic When a healthy baby cries inconsolably, usually in the late afternoon or evening every day, the baby may have colic. No one knows what causes colic, but it is temporary and harmless.

Do your best to soothe your baby by feeding, burping, changing, swaddling, rocking, etc. Try to conserve your energy and nap when the baby naps.

Before you assume that your baby has colic, let your baby's health care provider make sure that there is not some physical cause for your baby's fussiness. (For more about fussy babies, see Shaken Baby Syndrome on this page and How to Calm a Crying Baby on page 9.)

Second Month

Growth and Development

Baby's weight/length: _____

❋ When lying on his stomach, baby can hold his head at a 45 degree angle for a few seconds.
❋ Baby begins to turn his head to look for sounds.
❋ Baby begins to stay awake for longer periods during the day.
❋ Baby may begin smiling.

*Don't worry about spoiling
your baby. She won't remember
anything but the love part.*

Sucking You may notice that your baby has found her finger or thumb to suck on, or readily takes a pacifier.

Babies will often suck, even when they are not hungry, as a way of comforting themselves. Sucking on a pacifier or thumb is not a sign of insecurity, hunger, or emotional problems; and will not damage the developing teeth unless it continues past two to three years of age.

If your baby uses a pacifier, here are some safety suggestions:

❋ Do not use a pacifier that comes apart.

❋ Make sure the base of the pacifier is at least one and a half inches wide to avoid choking.

❋ Never tie a pacifier on a string around your baby's neck.

(Attach a photo of you and your baby here.)

---

*There's good news about
breast-feeding for moms, too.*

Nursing mothers should weigh five to ten pounds more than their ideal weight to maintain healthy milk production. Your daily requirement for calories has increased dramatically, so this is not the time to think about serious dieting.

Nursing mothers require 1,200 mg. of calcium a day and many health care providers recommend continuing with prenatal vitamins. You should continue to eat well-balanced meals and drink plenty of fluids to replace those lost in your breast milk. A good way to remember to drink enough is to have a glass of water every time you nurse your baby.

Be aware that any medicine you take, or alcohol you drink, will be present in your breast milk. If you have any questions about breast-feeding, ask your baby's health care provider.

---

*You want everything soft
and cuddly, except in the crib.*

Safety One of the most important jobs parents have is keeping their children safe. Here is the first of several safety checklists:

❋ Always keep the side rails up on your baby's crib. Traditional drop-side cribs have been deemed unsafe and are no longer sold. (See more at CPSC.gov.)

❋ Don't put the baby on or near any type of pillow or soft bedding — babies can get caught in bedding and suffocate.

❋ Don't leave the baby unattended on a table, couch, or bed, even briefly.

❋ Don't drink hot liquids while holding the baby.

❋ Install smoke detectors in your home.

❋ Introduce your baby to a playpen or play yard if you plan on using one. (See page 19.)

❋ When bathing your baby, test the water with your fingers to make sure it's not too hot before you put the baby in.

❋ Never leave your baby alone in the bath, even in shallow water.

❋ Do not accidentally leave your baby in a parked car. "Look before you lock" to prevent child heatstroke deaths in cars. (See more at KidsAndCars.org.)

Hand Washing Good hand washing is one of the most simple and effective ways to keep germs from infecting your family. Get into the habit of washing your hands frequently for at least ten to 15 seconds with an antibacterial soap and warm water. When your child is old enough, teach her to do the same.

Always wash your hands before feeding your baby, and after changing her diaper or using the bathroom. To further reduce the spread of germs, wash your child's toys regularly with warm, soapy water.

Third Month

This calendar gives general information on the events taking place during a baby's first year of life. It is not intended to take the place of your baby's health care. If you have any questions or concerns regarding your baby's health, call your baby's health care provider.

Be brave!
Taking a temperature
isn't hard or icky.

How to Take a Temperature Fever is the body's normal response to illness and is helpful in fighting infections. If your baby feels warm and you suspect a fever, take your baby's temperature. The most common ways to take a temperature are orally (in the mouth), axillary (under the armpit), rectally (in the rectum), and tympanic (in the ear).

For infants, a rectal temperature is the most accurate. Ear thermometers are not accurate until your baby is at least six months old. To take a rectal temperature, use this procedure:

1. Clear the digital thermometer.
2. Lubricate the thermometer with petroleum jelly.
3. Take the baby's diaper off.
4. Lay the child across your lap.
5. Spread the child's buttocks. Don't blindly poke — you could injure your baby.
6. Insert the thermometer about one inch into the rectum, but don't force it.
7. Hold your child still and press the buttocks together to stabilize the thermometer.
8. Hold the thermometer steady and leave it in for two to three minutes, or until it beeps. Then remove it.

Go to HealthyChildren.org to learn more about taking a child's temperature.

You can always call
your baby's health care provider
if you are unsure what to do.

Your baby doesn't need words
to tell you when he's not feeling well.

It can be difficult to know when your baby is sick. Try to become aware of your baby's normal sleeping and eating patterns and general disposition, so that you can detect a change early. Some signs of illness are:

❋ Irritability
❋ A high-pitched or constant cry
❋ Sleeping for an unusually long period of time
❋ Poor feeding or refusal to eat
❋ Diarrhea and/or vomiting
❋ Cold signs or symptoms
❋ Temperature of 100°F or higher (rectally) in an infant under two months old
❋ Temperature of 101°F or higher (rectally) in an infant over two months old

(Attach a photo of your baby smiling here.)

Fourth Month Checkup Once again it is time for your baby's well child checkup. These exams are vital to your baby's health because they allow your baby's health care provider to see your baby regularly and detect any health concerns early.

At the Fourth Month Checkup, your baby will be weighed and measured, and receive another set of immunizations. Have your baby care questions ready!

Non-Aspirin The American Academy of Pediatrics recommends that children and young adults through the age of 21 not be given aspirin, but a non-aspirin fever control medicine such as acetaminophen (like Tylenol), if they have any signs or symptoms of a viral illness such as sore throat, cough, cold, or chicken pox.

Acetaminophen is usually the first medication of choice for treating a fever. If the fever does not come down with acetaminophen, your baby's health care provider may recommend giving the baby a bath. Always consult your baby's health care provider for the appropriate dose and read the label carefully.

Ibuprofen, another type of fever reducer, should not be given to babies under six months of age.

If your baby is under four months old, do not give him any medication without the advice of his health care provider.

Fourth Month

Well Child Appointment

❋ Fourth Month Checkup:

❋ Questions to ask:

Growth and Development   Baby's weight/length: _____

❋ Baby becomes much more social this month and may start laughing.
❋ When on his stomach, baby can hold his head up well and pushes up on his arms.
❋ Baby may begin "batting" and kicking at toys.
❋ Baby's eyesight has improved and baby can focus at different distances.

Language and Hearing Good hearing enables a child to develop speech and language. A baby must be able to hear language repeatedly in order to learn how to speak. Researchers have found that the more a mother talks to her baby, the more words her baby knows!

Before birth, babies can hear and they begin to recognize certain sounds, especially their mother's voice. By two months of age, babies begin to turn their heads to look for sounds; and by three months, they begin to gurgle and coo.

By five months, your baby should be gurgling, cooing, and laughing when you laugh. You will notice her making vowel sounds like "ooh" and "aah." This early speech is a sign that your baby can hear. Other signs are startling to a loud noise and responding to the sound of your voice, even when you're out of the room.

If your baby isn't doing these things and you suspect a hearing problem, talk to your baby's health care provider and have your child tested by a hearing specialist (audiologist). Early discovery and treatment of hearing loss is vital to your baby's speech and language development.

Diaper Rash It is not unusual for babies to develop a rash in the diaper area. To treat diaper rash, try to keep the baby's skin as dry as possible. When she goes down for a nap, put her on top of a diaper, not in one. Banish baby wipes until the rash has cleared and use plain, warm water on a soft washcloth instead. Wash the diaper area gently and pat dry. Use zinc oxide, not powder. Call your baby's health care provider, if:

* The rash isn't better after treatment.
* The baby has a fever.
* The skin becomes blistered.
* The baby has white patches in her mouth or the diaper rash is bright red. (This could be a sign of a yeast infection which needs to be treated with a special ointment.)

Out of reach, out of mouth.

Now that your baby is more interested in her surroundings, you will notice that she reaches out for things and puts everything into her mouth. Here are some checks for child-proofing your home:

* Keep sharp objects such as pens, scissors, and safety pins out of baby's reach.
* Watch for small objects such as buttons, coins, and hard candy that baby could choke on.
* Cover electrical outlets.
* Keep all cords well out of baby's reach, including electrical cords, curtain pulls, and mobiles.
* Get into the habit of turning pot handles to the back of the stove.

How to Calm a Crying Baby The first and most important step in calming a crying baby is to respond to her, usually by picking her up. Responding to your baby allows her to form a healthy attachment to you and gives her a sense of security.

Next, try to determine if there's a physical reason for your baby's crying. Is she wet? Hungry? Too hot? Too cold? Does she need to be burped or have gas pains? (See the common signs of illness on page 7.)

If your baby seems to be okay, try swaddling her in a receiving blanket and holding her close, while walking with her or rocking her. Talk or sing to her softly. Offer her a pacifier. Consider taking her out for a ride in the car or a walk in the stroller.

If your baby is still crying and nothing you have tried is working, it is best to place her in a crib (or a playpen or infant seat) and walk away. It is perfectly fine to let a baby cry alone. In fact, the biggest threat to a crying baby is a caregiver who might hurt a baby out of anger or frustration. (See SBS on page 3.)

Health care professionals believe that robust crying bouts are normal and even healthy! Learn more at PurpleCrying.info and CalmACryingBaby.org. Here are the facts about normal crying:

* Babies can cry a lot — up to four to five hours a day!
* Babies communicate by crying.
* Babies cry more often in the evenings.
* Babies cry more often, starting at about two months old, and peaking at about five to six months old.
* Crying bouts can last over 30 to 40 minutes.
* Crying bouts can start or stop for no apparent reason.

Sleeping Your baby may be sleeping through the night now, or at least waking up less frequently. If your baby should wake up crying during the night, try not to give her a bottle in bed. This is known to promote both ear infections and tooth decay ("baby bottle caries"). When milk and juice sit in the mouth for long periods of time, the sugars in them can cause tooth decay. Even if your baby is just showing little tooth buds, she's at risk.

Fifth Month

Allergies When introducing new foods, try starting with one new food every five to seven days, watching for allergies. Some foods thought to cause allergies more than others are: wheat, citrus, egg whites, berries, nut butters, and seafood. Avoid these foods until your baby is nine to 12 months old, especially if you have a family history of allergies. Also avoid honey for the first year, because it has been associated with botulism in infants. If you have any questions or concerns about allergies or your baby's diet, discuss them with your baby's health care provider.

Juice Many babies love fruit juice and it is a nice addition to formula or breast milk, but should not be a substitute. Try to choose juice that is 100% natural and pasteurized. Until your baby is at least one year old, you will have to dilute it because juice, even if it's natural, is high in sugar and may cause diarrhea. If the juice is clear (like apple juice), dilute it with two parts of water to one part juice. If it's dark (like grape juice), dilute it four to one.

Teething A baby's first tooth usually erupts on the lower jaw between six and ten months of age, but some children won't get their first tooth until one year old. You will probably notice an increase in saliva (and drooling) when your child begins teething, and his gums may be slightly swollen and tender. Most children only experience mild discomfort with teething.

Chewing is your baby's natural way to relieve teething pain, so keep plenty of teething rings and cold washcloths on hand. Massaging tender gums with your finger may help and medicating with the appropriate dose of a non-aspirin medication is okay, too.

As soon as a tooth erupts, it's time to clean it! For the first year, you can "brush" your baby's teeth and gums by wiping them with a clean washcloth. A good time to do this is in the evening as part of your baby's bedtime routine.

Bon appetite, little baby.

Solid food.

So that's what those new teeth are for!

At six months of age, you may want to start introducing your baby to solid foods. Ideally, babies do not need solid foods before then, because breast milk and formula are still the best sources of nutrition and calories. Introduce new foods slowly and consult with your baby's health care provider. (See Allergies.)

First Solid Foods

Date :	Food Tried :	Reaction :

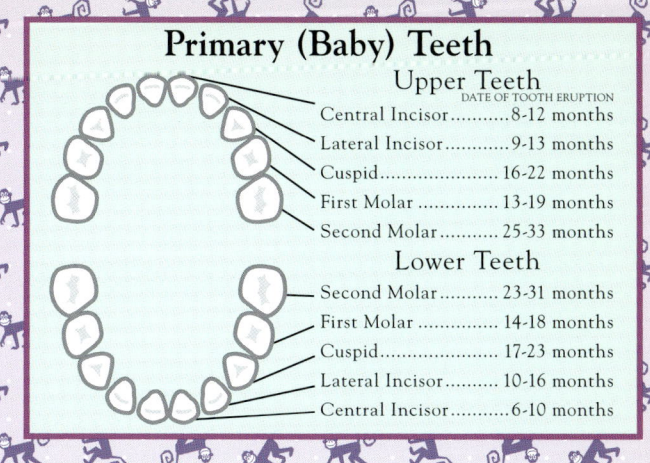

Primary (Baby) Teeth

Upper Teeth

DATE OF TOOTH ERUPTION

Central Incisor	8-12 months
Lateral Incisor	9-13 months
Cuspid	16-22 months
First Molar	13-19 months
Second Molar	25-33 months

Lower Teeth

Second Molar	23-31 months
First Molar	14-18 months
Cuspid	17-23 months
Lateral Incisor	10-16 months
Central Incisor	6-10 months

The Sixth Month Checkup is due, and so is another set of immunizations. Along with the shots, your baby will be weighed and measured. Your baby's health care provider will ask you questions about your baby's development and talk to you about solid foods. Have your questions ready, too!

First Foods Here are some good first solid foods to serve your baby, cooked and puréed:

* Rice cereal
* Oatmeal
* Carrots
* Squash
* Applesauce
* Bananas
* Peaches
* Pears
* Sweet potatoes

(Attach a photo of your baby enjoying a new treat here.)

Sixth Month

Growth and Development

Baby's weight/length: _____

❋ Baby will begin to sit more upright, but may still need support.
❋ Baby will begin rolling from back to stomach.
❋ Baby may begin transferring objects from hand to hand.
❋ Baby may begin babbling a string of sounds together.

Think Ahead The leading cause of death in children under five is accidental injury. The best protection against accidental injury (and poisoning) is prevention. Keeping a close eye on your baby and childproofing your home are important preventative measures. You should also know ahead of time what to do in an emergency. Prepare yourself by:

❋ Posting emergency numbers by all your phones.
❋ Taking an infant CPR (cardiopulmonary resuscitation) class and familiarizing yourself with the "Emergency Treatment for the Choking Infant" chart by the American Red Cross and American Heart Association.
❋ Taking a first aid course offered by the Red Cross.

If your child is seriously injured or choking, do not drive to the emergency room yourself, but call 911 or an ambulance.

Baby's Word Search Find as many words as you can related to babies. Words read across, up, down, diagonally, and backwards.

A	Q	B	A	B	Y	P	R	O	O	F	I	N	G	D
J	C	R	E	E	P	I	N	G	D	P	B	I	B	E
U	R	E	P	Y	N	N	A	N	T	R	Z	W	C	G
M	U	Q	T	K	I	S	S	I	P	U	E	I	R	R
P	I	Y	R	A	H	E	V	T	K	B	P	I	P	I O
E	S	R	E	A	M	U	K	N	Q	O	U	E	B	G
R	I	G	S	D	S	I	G	U	C	N	D	S	V	N
X	N	N	I	A	Z	P	N	B	O	N	E	S	I	E
S	G	I	C	H	I	B	B	O	P	E	H	H	P	L
L	Z	T	R	R	W	Y	M	E	P	T	C	O	E	U
E	W	T	E	A	A	T	S	M	R	H	S	T	C	L
E	E	A	X	T	L	O	H	S	C	R	E	S	A	L
P	A	B	E	T	K	O	P	V	U	J	I	N	C	A
E	N	M	C	L	E	P	A	C	I	F	I	E	R	B
R	O	M	P	E	R	T	B	U	M	P	E	R	S	Y

WORDS TO FIND:

acetaminophen	burp	exercise	nanny	romper
babyproofing	colic	fussy	OPV	schedule
batting	creeping	HIB	onesie	shots
bib	crib	hug	pacifier	sleeper
bonnet	cruising	jumper	pins	walker
bumpers	DTP	kiss	raspberries	wean
bunting	engorged	lullaby	rattle	wipes

There's no such thing as an overprotective parent, not the first year. Or the second or the third…

At about seven months, you'll notice a big difference in how much more active your baby is. Her arms, legs, and body are moving all the time. Although she may not be crawling yet, it's amazing how quickly she gets around just by scooting or "creeping."

Follow this checklist to make your home as safe as possible:

❋ Place a sturdy gate at the top and bottom of stairways.
❋ Keep doors leading outside or to a basement closed and secured with an extra latch up high.
❋ Install baby locks on cabinets that contain unsafe things.
❋ Install window guards on upper floors.
❋ Remove baby's mobile from her crib, if you haven't already.
❋ Baby will try to grab your hot cup of coffee or tea.
❋ Keep plastic bags, polystyrene packing material, and balloons out of baby's reach, as well as any small object that baby could put in her mouth and choke on.

Poisonous Plants There are many poisonous plants; some are common house plants, others may be growing in your yard or favorite park. To prevent plant poisonings, follow these guidelines from the Rocky Mountain Poison Control Center:

1. Never let your children eat stems, leaves, berries, nuts, or seeds from any plant.
2. Obtain a list of poisonous plants from your baby's health care provider or poison control center.
3. Know the botanical names of your house and yard plants.
4. Store bulbs and seeds in a safe place.
5. Never assume a plant is safe to eat because birds or animals eat it.
6. If you think your child has eaten a poisonous plant, follow the instructions below.

Poisonings If you suspect your child has eaten or drunk something poisonous and she is having difficulty breathing, is drooling, having convulsions, or seems sleepy, call 911 or an ambulance immediately. If she does not appear to be ill, call your poison control center immediately for instructions. Until you have received instructions, do not give anything by mouth, including syrup of ipecac. Your poison control center will advise you on whether or not to make your child vomit. Save the bottle the poison was in and take it with you if you must go to the emergency room.

Emergency Phone Numbers

In case of an emergency, call 911 or:

Emergency Ambulance:

Poison Control Center:

Baby's Health Care Provider:

Pharmacy:

Police:

Fire Dept.:

Neighbor or Relative:

Your Address and Phone Number:

Seventh Month

Beware of Choking Choking is a constant threat to small children, especially babies who are just starting to eat solid foods. Always watch your child during mealtimes, and warn older children not to share their food with the baby.

Here is a list of foods to avoid:

❋ Nuts of any kind	❋ Hard candy
❋ Seeds of any kind	❋ Popcorn
❋ Raisins	❋ Gum
❋ Raw vegetables	❋ Marshmallows

Always chop into small pieces before serving:

❋ Hot dogs	❋ Grapes
❋ Sausage	

Become familiar with the "Emergency Treatment for the Choking Infant" chart by the American Red Cross and American Heart Association.

Constipation occurs when a child has hard stools, causing it to hurt when he has a bowel movement.

Chances are it's your baby's diet that is causing the problem. Foods such as rice cereal, bananas, applesauce, cheese, and pasta can be constipating. Try reducing these foods and replacing them with foods that are high in fiber such as strained apricots, prunes, pears, or peaches at least two times a day. A serving of fruit juice may also help.

Call your baby's health care provider if:

❋ Even after you change your baby's diet, he is still having hard, painful stools.
❋ Your child has severe abdominal pain or cramping.
❋ Blood is present in the stool.

Do not give suppositories or an enema to your baby without the advice of your baby's health care provider.

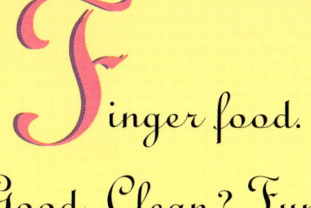

Finger food. Good. Clean? Fun!

At about eight months, most babies become very interested in food and enjoy playing with it as much as eating it. Although mealtimes can be messy, try to encourage this independence by giving your baby finger foods.

First Finger Foods

Date :	Food Tried :	Reaction :

Diarrhea is the sudden passing of loose, watery bowel movements more frequently than usual. Diarrhea is usually caused by a viral infection of the intestine and can last from several days to one week, regardless of the treatment.

The best treatment for mild diarrhea is to keep the baby well-hydrated by giving plenty of fluids. If the baby is taking solid foods, change the diet. Place your baby on a diet of constipating foods such as applesauce, strained bananas, rice, and rice cereal. Do not give the baby any fruit juice, but continue with breast- or formula-feedings.

Keep in mind that a severe case of diarrhea in infants can be life-threatening. If your baby has any of the following signs of severe diarrhea or dehydration, call your baby's health care provider immediately:

❋ Loose, watery bowel movements every one or two hours.
❋ Blood present in the bowel movement.
❋ Your baby vomits or refuses to eat or drink.
❋ Your baby hasn't urinated in the past eight hours.
❋ Crying produces no tears and baby's mouth is dry.
❋ Fever of 101°F or higher (rectally) in a baby over two months old. (For a baby under two months old, see First Checkups on page 1.)
❋ Baby appears to be in pain or is acting sick.

Do not give the baby any anti-diarrhea medication unless directed by your baby's health care provider.

Finger Foods should be bite-sized, easy to pick up, and easy to swallow. Some good first finger foods are dry cereal (like Cheerios), cooked peas, and soft, ripe bananas, peaches, pears, and melon. Dice the fruit into small cubes. You may also start giving your baby table foods such as mashed potatoes, cooked vegetables, and cooked meat, as long as they are cut into little pieces.

Eighth Month

Child Care Checklist

Baby's Name:

Date of Birth:

Allergies:

Special Instructions:

Home Address:

Parents' Names and Phone Numbers:

Baby's Health Care Provider:

Neighbor or Relative:

Stranger Anxiety About this time some babies experience "stranger anxiety." You'll know that your baby has it when a friend or relative tries to hold her and your sweet, sociable baby suddenly clings to you and won't let go! Don't despair, this reaction to strangers (or even to those who aren't strangers) is a normal part of your baby's growth and development, and it will pass.

Your baby is simply becoming more attached to you and feels insecure when another person comes too close.

It is best to reassure your baby and allow her the time she needs to feel comfortable, even if it means asking someone to wait a little bit before holding her.

Security Blanket You may have noticed that your baby has become very attached to a certain toy, stuffed animal, or blanket. One way that a baby copes with anxiety is to develop an attachment to a security object. This special object works like magic to soothe, calm, and comfort your baby.

Don't worry, attachment to a security object is normal and most children outgrow them between the ages of three and six.

Your baby has a favorite toy. You.

Researchers have found that a baby's relationship with its parents and caregivers can have a big effect on brain development. The best thing that parents can do for their children is to give them consistent, loving care so that they are able to form secure attachments. It's not necessary to buy expensive toys or apps to stimulate brain development. Just give your baby the attention she needs and plenty of opportunities for fun and play. Set healthy limits on screen time. "Talk time" and "face time" with you is much more important! It won't be long before your baby grabs your cell phone, so develop good habits and routines now!

Favorite Activities

The Ninth Month Checkup is here already! Your baby's health care provider may draw some blood from your baby to check for anemia. It may be time for another set of immunizations depending on your child's schedule.

Once again your baby will be weighed and measured, and your baby's health care provider will discuss her eating habits and development with you. Have your questions ready!

Promoting Young Children's Healthy Development:

1. Be warm, loving, and responsive.
2. Respond to your child's cues and clues.
3. Talk, read, and sing to your child.
4. Establish routines and rituals.
5. Encourage safe exploration and play.
6. Make TV watching selective (and limit all screen time).
7. Use discipline as an opportunity to teach.
8. Recognize that each child is unique.
9. Choose quality child care and stay involved.
10. Take care of yourself.

Ninth Month

Well Child Appointment

❋ Ninth Month Checkup:

❋ Questions to ask:

Growth and Development   Baby's weight/length: _____

❋ Baby begins pulling to a stand, but may have trouble getting back down.
❋ Baby enjoys crawling up stairs.
❋ Baby knows her name and turns her head when she hears it.
❋ Baby is beginning to understand simple words like "no" and "stop!"

Even someone who can't stand up yet can still fall down a lot.

Ouch! Scrapes, bumps, and bruises come with the territory as your baby practices newfound skills. So it's important to know basic first aid. First aid for minor scrapes and cuts involves looking closely at the wound, and then washing it with warm, soapy water. This may take some determination on your part because your baby won't like it.

If you're not sure whether or not stitches are needed, call your baby's health care provider. Do not wait too long to have a cut looked at, because after a period of time it may be too late to stitch. This is particularly important if the cut is on your baby's face.

If your baby is up-to-date on all immunizations, it won't be necessary to get a tetanus shot.

Baby's First Bump

(Attach a photo of your baby with a favorite book here.)

*R*eading to your baby is *quality time of the highest quality!*

It's never too early to show your baby a picture book and start reading together. It will enhance his vocabulary, language, and speech development. Hearing your voice and speech patterns will also help to shape and develop the language areas of your child's brain.

Try to read to your child daily, choosing books with colorful pictures. Point to the things you are reading about and repeat their names. Vary the tone of your voice and ask questions to encourage your baby's participation. Read favorites over and over again. Although it may seem a little boring to you, children learn from repetition.

Favorite Books

A Playpen (play yard or portable crib) offers a safe place for your baby to play or sleep in, and perhaps a short break for you. Playpens can be invaluable when visiting friends and relatives, because they instantly provide a childproofed area. Use these guidelines for safe playpen use:

✳ *Place the playpen in a safe, open area so that baby cannot reach out to something dangerous.*

✳ *Only put safe toys in with the baby and discourage other children from giving their toys to the baby.*

✳ *Do not attach anything to the playpen with a string or ribbon.*

✳ *Check the playpen for compliance with safety standards. (Go to CPSC.gov.)*

✳ *Check that there is not a gap between the mattress and the playpen sides for baby to get caught in.*

✳ *Check for any sharp hardware or edges.*

✳ *If your mesh playpen is designed to have one side drop down, do not leave the side dropped down while your baby is in the playpen. It could entrap him and cause suffocation.*

✳ *Check for overall stability. The playpen should have sturdy locks to prevent a child from collapsing it.*

While playpens offer many benefits, babies still need to be given the freedom to crawl around and explore.

Weaning You may continue to breast-feed as long as you like—don't feel you must begin weaning when your baby starts teething and eating solid foods. However, once your baby develops a taste for certain solid foods, he may be less interested in breast-feeding.

Some women begin weaning by replacing one breast-feeding session (say at lunchtime) with a meal of solid foods and a bottle or cup. Then a week or two later, if all is going well, eliminate a second breast-feeding session, and so on. Take it at your baby's pace. The early morning and late evening feedings will be the last to go.

Tenth Month

Growth and Development

Baby's weight/length: ______________

- Baby may begin "cruising" furniture.
- When holding onto furniture, baby may stoop or squat to pick up a toy.
- Baby may begin "walking" if both hands are held.
- Baby enjoys listening to rhymes and songs.

Sleep, the impossible dream?

(Attach a photo of your baby sleeping here.)

An Ear Infection is an infection in the middle ear space behind the eardrum. It may be difficult to tell if your baby has an ear infection; symptoms include irritability, fever, and staying awake more than usual at night.

If you suspect an ear infection, call your baby's health care provider for an appointment. Many ear infections will need to be treated with antibiotics. If left untreated, your child's hearing could be damaged. Earaches are usually very painful.

Your child will be scheduled for a follow-up appointment about two weeks later to make sure the infection is gone. Keep this appointment even if you think your child is better!

Baby's First Illness

What every parent finds out about toys : Babies are just as happy playing with the box.

Toys are great fun and provide lots of stimulation for your baby. Choose toys that are brightly colored and have different textures. Remember, toys don't have to be expensive or new to be interesting to a baby. Babies love banging on pots and pans, and playing with cups, boxes, and large spoons. Before you give your baby a toy, consider these safety tips:

* *Avoid toys with small parts that baby could choke on.*
* *Never allow children to play with balloons unsupervised or put them in their mouths.*
* *Many toys have a suggested age category printed on their packaging. Keep toys for older children away from baby.*

Long naps can make for long nights.

Sleeping Morning and afternoon naps are good for most babies this age, but try to keep naps under two hours to avoid late night wakefulness.

Most parents find it best to have a consistent bed-time routine. You should establish one ending with a good night kiss, then leave your baby to fall asleep on her own. After a busy day, most babies will be ready to go to sleep at bedtime.

Remember that as your baby grows or gets a new tooth, her sleeping pattern may change—a baby who has been sleeping through the night may begin to wake-up during the night again.

Time for Milk? At about one year old, many babies can start drinking regular cow's milk. Your baby's health care provider will advise you on how and when to make the switch, and what type of milk product to use.

The change in diet should be gradual to make sure that your baby can tolerate milk. Some signs of milk intolerance are:

* *Vomiting*
* *Abdominal pain, cramping, or gas*
* *Diarrhea or constipation*
* *Refusal to eat*

If your baby has any of these symptoms or appears uncomfortable, call your baby's health care provider.

Vitamins Many parents worry about whether or not their baby needs a vitamin supplement when their baby stops taking breast milk or formula. The best source of vitamins is a healthy diet that includes plenty of green and yellow vegetables, fresh or canned fruit, and protein such as milk, fish, meat, poultry, and beans. If you are concerned about your baby's diet, ask your baby's health care provider to recommend a vitamin supplement.

Eleventh Month

Water Safety Drowning can occur in any amount of water if it covers the nose and mouth. So take special care around even the smallest amounts of water, including pails of water, dog bowls, fish tanks, fountains, wading pools, sinks, and toilets.

* Never leave young children alone in the bathtub or bathroom.
* Never leave water in the tub or sink.
* Keep toilet lids down.
* Empty water buckets when not in use.
* Keep toddlers away from pools.
* Deflate small pools when not in use and turn them over so rain cannot collect in them.
* Teach your children to swim when they are old enough.

Sun Protection Protect your baby from sunburn because every childhood sunburn increases his chance of getting skin cancer as an adult. The sun's harmful, invisible UV (ultraviolet) rays can also cause dry, wrinkled, and prematurely-aged skin.

Try to avoid having your baby out in direct sunlight during its most harmful hours between 10:00 a.m. and 3:00 p.m. If you must be out at that time, follow the four rules of the "Slip, Slop, Slap, and Wrap" skin cancer prevention campaign:

1. Slip on a loose-fitting cotton shirt.
2. Slop on sunscreen with SPF 30 and UVA/UVB protection.
3. Slap on a broad-brimmed hat.
4. Wrap on sunglasses to protect your eyes and the surrounding sensitive skin.

And don't forget the lip balm with sunscreen!

Those first steps can happen any day now. You'd better be quick to keep up.

(Attach a photo of your one-year-old here)

What an amazing year. But wait, it gets better.

As your baby's first birthday gets closer, you may notice that he seems to understand what you're saying to him. And he does!

Babies probably understand 100 words for every one they speak, so keep talking to your baby and involving him in your conversations and you will be giving his language development a big boost.

Most babies say their first word by one year of age. By 18 months, their vocabulary will grow to about 20 words; and by two years old, they'll begin putting two words together. Sentences of three or more words usually begin between the ages of two and three.

First Words

Walking Most babies begin to walk by themselves between nine and 15 months old. At first your baby's steps will be awkward, with feet wide apart and arms held high for balance. You'll also notice a big grin on his face as he masters this newfound skill.

Your baby will topple over easily while he is learning to walk, and it is important to guard against falls on hard surfaces. With gentle encouragement and handholding, he will gradually lower his arms and bring his feet closer together. Before you know it, he'll be walking entirely on his own!

The Twelfth Month Checkup is here! After your baby has been weighed and measured, be sure to ask your child's health care provider if any immunizations are due.

Keep in mind that there are more well child checkups to come. They are due at 15 to 18 months, and at 24 months. After that, your child should have a physical exam once every year.

Twelfth Month

Well Child Appointment

❊ Twelfth Month Checkup:

❊ Questions to ask:

Growth and Development   Baby's weight/length: _____

❊ Baby may start using one word correctly besides "ma-ma" and "da-da."
❊ Baby may begin responding to simple requests like giving up a toy
   when asked.
❊ Baby makes you very aware of his likes and dislikes.
❊ Baby may take a few steps alone. A few babies will be walking now.

Baby's Crossword Puzzle *

ACROSS

1. Protects baby in crib
5. This cutie is a new walker.
10. __ apple a day
11. Time and a half (abbr.)
13. Electric Light Orchestra (abbr.)
14. _____ as sugar
16. Baby's searching for her mother's nipple
19. Baby's first bathtub
20. Baby's first food
21. Jack __ the box
22. Presently
24. What water does at low tide
27. Bismarck is its capital. (abbr.)
28. I'll __ seeing you.
29. Masculine form of ma'am
30. __ Golden Pond
31. ___ much did he weigh?
32. Born before the 37th week
35. Husband, baby, and you
36. Place to mail letters from (abbr.)
37. Cigar residue
38. Above all, stay ____!
40. You and me
42. What you may desperately crave
43. Pavarotti was a _____.
44. Two-year-old's favorite word
45. Leisure suits, mood rings, and pet rocks
46. Te ___ means 'I love you' in Spanish
47. Weak
50. Computer on the go
52. To wrap a baby snugly with a receiving blanket
54. What is your baby's ___?
55. Immunizations
56. Breast-feeding

DOWN

1. Baby's first bed
2. Do this at day's end
3. Baby's favorite game
4. Early in nursing, mothers often suffer these. (2 words)
6. Come ___ and play!
7. Not fake (abbr.)
8. Above-ground train (abbr.)
9. Baby's first pony (2 words)
12. __ grandmother's house we go!
15. Printer's measure
17. At 40 weeks, what you feel, but you're not.
18. Santa Fe is its capital. (abbr.)
23. Not old
25. Used to control a horse
26. Used to absorb milk (2 words)
31. A vaccination (abbr.)
33. Baby's one-piece outfits
34. Most important
38. Demands
39. Moral storyteller
40. Baby's mother's and father's brothers
41. __ it goes!
42. A tiff
47. A lion's den
48. Doctor (abbr.)
49. Panache
51. Opposite of con
53. The sperm and the ___

* Answers to the puzzles can be found at BabysFirstYear.com/answers

---

Baby's Keepsake Page

My name is

I was born on _____ at _____ a.m./p.m.

at the

I weighed _____ pounds, _____ ounces; and measured _____ inches from head to toe.

My eyes were _____, my hair was

Everyone said I resembled

My parents are

My grandparents are

and

My first home was at

I have an older brother named

I have an older sister named

I have a pet named

Some things that were happening around the world when I was born

---

Your Child's Immunization Record

Name:

Date of Birth:

Vaccine:	Date:	Dose Number				
		1	2	3	4	5